BY MARY FLEESON

Faith is perhaps one of the
most challenging concepts to
understand and to practice.
Let us explore together what a
difference faith makes...

And now these three remain: faith, hope and love.

How do we say with confidence "I believe"? How do we calm the waves of doubt and quiet the persistent babble of fears that tell us that our faith is just something someone invented to satisfy a need and give some kind of meaning to our existence...

The absolute answer may be different for each of us, we may have experienced answers to prayer, seen miracles, been brought up in an environment where faith was a normal part of daily life, met God through the actions of others or you may have read the Bible and something about it just made sense. Even through your doubts and fears say out loud, "Lord, I believe."

Try repeating the words as you colour them in on the opposite page

SO THEN, JUST AS YOU RECEIVED CHRIST JESUS AS LORD, CONTINUE TO LIVE YOUR LIVES IN HIM, ROOTED AND BUILT UP IN HIM, STRENGTHENED IN THE FAITH AS YOU WERE TAUGHT, AND OVERFLOWING WITH THANKFULNESS.
Colossians 2 6-7

EVEN YOUTHS GROW TIRED AND WEARY, AND YOUNG MEN STUMBLE AND FALL; BUT THOSE WHO HOPE IN THE LORD WILL RENEW THEIR STRENGTH. THEY WILL SOAR ON WINGS LIKE EAGLES; THEY WILL RUN AND NOT GROW WEARY, THEY WILL WALK AND NOT BE FAINT.
Isaiah 40 30-31

The image opposite, 'Faith, Hope and Eternal Love', was inspired, initially, by the idea that a tree that offered shelter to a parent and baby could become the cross that held Jesus and then a symbol of faith, of hope and of love. The purpose of that tree in life, rooted deep in the earth, fruitful and useful, is no less important in death when it became a cross. The tree didn't get a say in its use or purpose but we do.

A deeply rooted faith blossoms when we choose daily to accept the challenge of living as Jesus taught; if our hopes rest in Gods hands our spirits are free to grow and thrive; an when we choose to see ou fellow humans through God's eyes perhaps we ca love them more fully and forgive them more freely.

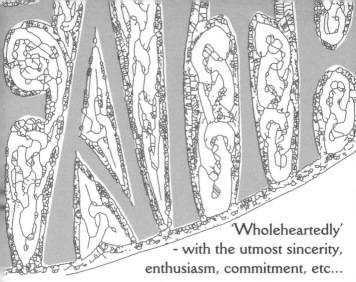

'Wholeheartedly'
- with the utmost sincerity, enthusiasm, commitment, etc...

I love words, I'm fascinated by their power and meaning, In the short prayer, 'Mighty God, help me to believe wholeheartedly', I wanted to use a word that was true to the power and meaning of faith, a word that left no doubt as to its intention or purpose. A Thesaurus gives us some other words and phrases that have the same, or a similar meaning.

Try replacing wholeheartedly with any of the words below and see if it changes your understanding of the prayer...

Mighty God help me to believe...

CANDIDLY	PROFOUNDLY	IN ALL CONSCIENCE
DEEPLY	TRULY	IN ALL SINCERITY
EARNESTLY	TRUTHFULLY	INGENUOUSLY
GENUINELY	IN GOOD FAITH	FROM BOTTOM OF HEART
NATURALLY	FRANKLY	WITHOUT EQUIVOCATION

The words by the unknown author of the letter to the Hebrews sum up the conundrum of faith, complete trust or confidence, in God.

Trying to explain faith beyond those words is difficult and yet a challenge most people with a belief will have to answer at some point. Wiser people than me have suggested ideas that may deepen our understanding…

Faith does not operate in the realm of the possible. There is no glory for God in that which is humanly possible. Faith begins where man's power ends.
George Mueller 1805-1898

Faith is like Wi-Fi, it's invisible but it has the power to connect you to the one who has everything that you need.
Anon.

and…

Faith is taking the first step even when you don't see the whole staircase.

Martin Luther King, Jr.

I'm sure I'm not the first person to be told that my faith, the thing that I have built my entire life on, is a delusion, it's been said with a sympathetic, indulgent smile as if I'm just a little lacking in working brain cells and also with the aggressive surety of someone who doubts that their own lack of faith is a better path. I haven't always responded gracefully, at least in private, I'm a work in progress, but the words that pop into my mind every time are 'Be still, and know that I am God.' As God spoke to David, the same God speaks to us today in every stressful and challenging situation...

Be still, and know' that I am God

Psalm 46:10

t's good to be challenged, faith can be a fragile thing f not reenforced by experience and action, and if we can't ell others of our personal experiences of God working n us how can we hope to share the good news of our Creator's love for all?

Abraham! "Here I am," he replied. Then God

"Take your son, your only son, whom you love –
– and go to the region of Moriah. Sacrifice him
as a burnt offering on a mountain I will show
Early the next morning Abraham got up and
ed his donkey. He took with him two of his
ants and his son Isaac. When he had cut enough
for the burnt offering, he set out for the place
had told him about. On the third day Abraham
ed up and saw the place in the distance. He said
s servants, "Stay here with the donkey while I
he boy go over there. We will worship and then
ill come back to you." Abraham took the wood
e burnt offering and placed it on his son Isaac,
he himself carried the fire and the knife. As the
f them went on together, Isaac spoke up and
o his father Abraham, "Father?" "Yes, my son?"
ham replied. "The fire and wood are here,"
said, "but where is the lamb for the burnt
ng?" Abraham answered, "God himself will
de the lamb for the burnt offering, my son." And
wo of them went on together. When they
ed the place God had told him about, Abraham
an altar there and arranged the wood on it. He
d his son Isaac and laid him on the altar, on top
e wood. Then he reached out his hand and took
nife to slay his son. But the angel of the Lord
d out to him from heaven, "Abraham! Abraham!"
I am," he replied. "Do not lay a hand on the
he said. "Do not do anything to him. Now I know
ou fear God, because you have not withheld
me your son, your only son." Abraham looked
d there in a thicket he saw a ram caught by its
. He went over and took the ram and sacrificed
a burnt offering instead of his son. So Abraham
that place The Lord Will Provide. And to this
is said, "On the mountain of the Lord it will be
led." The angel of the Lord called to Abraham
heaven a second time and said, "I swear by
lf, declares the Lord, that because you have
this and have not withheld your son, your only
I will surely bless you and make your
endants as numerous as the stars in the sky
s the sand on the seashore. Your descendants
ke possession of the cities of their enemies,
rough your offspring all nations on earth will be

I'm not sure I have that much faith... not as much as Abraham. I suspect that for most modern people of faith the request from any god to sacrifice a human, let alone ones own child, would be a deal-breaker in terms of continuing to follow that god. I can't pretend to truly understand cultures where the sacrifice of living creatures is an acceptable form of devotion, except in an historical and cultural context, but Abraham's story serves as a powerful reminder that faith and sacrifice are often closely intertwined.

What have you sacrificed for your faith?

"Therefore I tell you, do not worry about your life, what you will eat or drink; or about your body, what you will wear. Is not life more than food, and the body more than clothes? Look at the birds of the air; they do not sow or reap or store away in barns, and yet your heavenly Father feeds them. Are you not much more valuable than they? Can any one of you by worrying add a single hour to your life? "And why do you worry about clothes? See how the flowers of the field grow. They do not labour or spin. Yet I tell you that not even Solomon in all his splendour was dressed like one of these. If that is how God clothes the grass of the field, which is here today and tomorrow is thrown into the fire, will he not much more clothe you - you of little faith? So do not worry, saying, 'What shall we eat?' or 'What shall we drink?' or 'What shall we wear?' ...

But seek first his kingdom and his righteousness and all these things will be given to you as well

THEREFORE DO NOT WORRY ABOUT TOMORROW. FOR TOMORROW WILL WORRY ABOUT ITSELF. EACH DAY HAS ENOUGH TROUBLE OF ITS OWN.

Matthew 6:25 - 3

When all seems black,
help me to live within
the joy of Your love.

When all seems dark,
help me to see clearly
the purity of Your light,

When all seems hopeless,
help me to remember easily
the hope of Your words.

When all seems discordant,
help me to identify, defiantly
the harmony of Your creation.

P
R
A
Y

AND MY GOD WILL MEET ALL YOUR
NEEDS ACCORDING TO THE RICHES
OF HIS GLORY IN CHRIST JESUS

Philippians 4:1

Lately I've discovered a new appreciation for Paul's letters; understanding that some of his more contentious teachings are simply a product of their time, I like how they show him to be a very 'warts and all' kind of human. In the apocryphal 'Acts of Paul' he is described as "a man little of stature, thin-haired upon the head, crooked in the legs, of good state of body, with eyebrows joining, and nose somewhat hooked, full of grace: for sometimes he appeared like a man, and sometimes he had the face of an angel."

There's plenty of theological debate to be had about Paul and the things that he said and was supposed to have said but perhaps his greatest gift to us today is his unapologetic faith. Knowing that others share our belief is crucial to our own faith and Paul is still offering us that reassurance today.

Think of the ways we share our faith today, what more can we do?

and suddenly there shined round about him a light from heaven
Acts 9v3

ALWAYS BE PREPARED TO GIVE AN ANSWER TO EVERYONE WHO ASKS YOU TO GIVE THE REASON FOR THE HOPE THAT YOU HAVE. BUT DO THIS WITH GENTLENESS AND RESPECT.
1 PETER 3:15

BUT AS FOR ME,
I WATCH IN HOPE
FOR THE LORD,
I WAIT FOR GOD
MY SAVIOUR:
MY GOD
WILL HEAR ME

PRAY

But as for me,

I watch in hope for the Lord,

Help me to accept the push that propels me into action.

Let my faith be enough for the tasks You have set before me

I wait for God my Saviour,

Help me to realise that my God is waiting patiently for me.

Let my faith be enough for the path You have shown me.

My God will hear me, but oh my God,

in the midst of my days, let me hear You.

Micah 7v7

PRAY

Circle me Creator God.
May I hope joyfully,
Keep me from despair.
May I love freely,
Keep me from indifference.
May I believe expectantly,
Keep me from ignorance.